*"All life has a right to be
nurtured, appreciated, valued
and respected,
and to be shown joy"*

© J M Loughrill

*"No one should pay a price emotionally, spiritually or physically for love, affection or friendship"*

# MY SILENT VOICES

J M LOUGHRILL

www.mysilentvoices.com

jmloughrill@hotmail.com

Book Cover & Design:
Thomas Monsen
thomasmonsen@me.com

ISBN 9781076841247

# DEDICATIONS

My parents Molly and Peter
for their gift of Life.

Aunt Lilly and Uncle Jim
for catching me when I could have fallen.

My siblings John, Joe, Peter, Betty and Helen.

My sons, Stuart and Ben.

My wife Maureen
for her love, support and encouragement,
particularly during my moments of self-inflicted chaos.

John Monks (Sparky).

My Friends in Spirit.

# ACKNOWLEDGEMENT

My thanks and gratitude to Norman Warwick,
author and co-founder of
'All Across The Arts' and 'Just Poets'
for his enthusiasm, support, patience
and guidance
in helping me to bring these words to fruition.
www.aata.dev

# FORWARD

The author was born in Southern Ireland. Orphaned at an early age he was taken to England where he began a colorful life as an Irish immigrant. Although he never knew his parents, he always had a sense of being watched over.

In later years, early one morning, he was drawn to his office where he typed a heading. "I Will Still Be". This was at a time when a close friend had passed away after a long illness and he was to attend the funeral in a few days. His eulogy was finished within a few minutes. After reading it through, it felt to him like a message from his late friend.

This was the beginning of many early morning awakenings, all following the same pattern of title, verse and, invariably, completion. These writings have brought to him support, guidance and comfort, and personal debate, leading to a fulfilling life.

The author would like to encourage you to make time for self, be still, and reach out to those loved ones in spirit who are watching over you. To listen for their silent voices offering you guidance and unconditional love.

# CONTENTS

# MY SILENT VOICES

A Spiritual Awakening
experienced through Verse

# I Will Still Be

In whispers of your life,
I will still be.

In your thoughts,
I will still be.

In a gentle breeze,
when you need me,
I will still be.

In a soft touch on your shoulder,
I will still be.

In your quiet moments,
I will still be.

In celebrations of your life,
I will still be.

In your dreams
as you sleep,
I will still be.

In your Love,
I will still be.

In your Peace,
I will still be.

In the presence
of those passed before me,
I will still be.

With you,
always.
I will still be.

# Endeavors

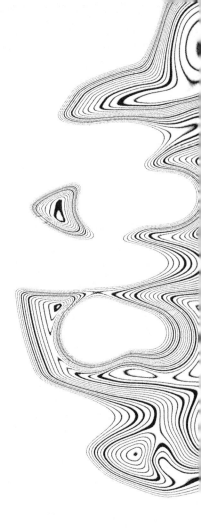

In your eyes, I see Truth.
In your voice, I hear Faith.
In your wisdom, I sense Guidance,

born with a gift, so strong, so rich,

with no knowledge of the course intended,
extremes of emotion lain bare,
and absorbed.

In the light of Learning
a gentle Soul emerges,
Truthful and Faithful.

In your deeds lay Compassion.
In your heart, true Love.
In your Soul, good Intent,
fused by pain.

With ego lain aside,
you listen
to silent voices,
guiding you to your higher self.

# Reaching Out

In your fear, I seem so distant,
as though you will never reach me.

Your inner resistance
my friend,
is not of any substance,
but, instead, created in absence of faith.

I have never betrayed you.
I ask now that you open to me.

Many years have passed.
Memories clouded.
Awaken, to fulfill your destiny.

Be not fearful.
As a child learns to walk,
so, you are learning to trust.

Ahead of you are the answers.
Follow your path intuitively.

Be alert,
you are being guided.
Be not doubtful of this.

I cannot yet be known to you.
I tell you now, friend,
we are not strangers.

Trust the signs you receive.
They are not fabrications of your mind.
Your senses are not deceiving you.
These are communications from me.

In Time they will, set you free.

Be not angry against yourself.
Be not impatient.
In Light will be
your Answer,
your Healing,
your Joy.

Swim not against currents of life,
but, instead, flow with them.

My friend,
you will be guided to waters
holding no danger for you.

In your place of meditation,
Spirit will be with you.
As you awash with awakening
your tears will flow.

Friend, be not afraid of this.

Each tear will carry
negativity into the mist.
Each tear will replenish you
with positive, loving thoughts.

Friend,
you will not be alone.
You have bountiful Spirit
with you on earth.

I will stand beside you, as always,
to your left.

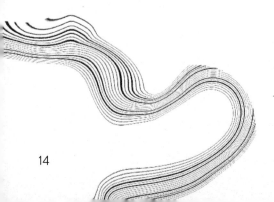

# Truth

In Truth is your Peace.
Friend be brave.
Do not fear Truth.
No harm will come upon you.
Love will be in abundance.

In this moment you feel my
presence.
You know this.
It is so,
yet you are not accepting.

In Time,
as you reflect, in your writings,
on
our connection, our voices,
your Trust will grow.

Do not fear Truth,
for I am with you.
I am close in this moment.

Friend, stay in Truth,
open to this moment.

What may divide us?

I am to your left.

We are One.

You shiver,
conscious of your heart.
You arose to write.
Trust in me.

We are, indeed,
closer than you know.

In Truth, you will see.
In Truth, you will be.
In Truth, you are free.

I am to your left.

We are closer.
You are embracing Wisdom.
The fruit will be yours.

No question.
No doubt.
One Truth.

Love will be in abundance.

# You And I Are One

Friend hear me.
Fear not.
You will achieve your Destiny.
In silent voices you will find Peace,
for you and I are one.

Your fear is not of now,
nor of this Time on earth.
Within,
you fear you cannot
follow the path agreed.

Within,
you fear the learning we agreed,
will not be fulfilled.

Fear not, friend.
You are not as far away as you feel.
You have no conflict with Soul.
Your Soul has Truth
and Truth will win through.

Stay with the journey of self.
Each turn will be guided.
Awakening, you feel confused.
Fear not,
for Love guides you clear.

For Spirit,
you have much work to do.
Friend, have no haste within you.

In the moment,
what has been decreed
will flow.

In the moment,
not before,
nor too late.

In the moment.

# Tragedy

In tragedy you may question
Validity, Truth and Reason.

In your perception of tragedy
ego is present.

Let all actions of Nature and Man
be
questioned, researched, explored.

In Light we see no tragedy.

In Light we experience
no judgment,
no guilt, retribution nor revenge.

Destiny hails no questions.

All is one and returns.

Where Time does not exist,
no boundaries are created.
In Spirit our carriage is Love.

All is one and returns.

Be free.
Time is of no consequence,
in past life or the next.

Heed not voices of others.
As you come closer to your true Destiny,
honor your work within.

Show compassion.
Protect yourself, my friend, with Light.
Enjoy your Freedom.
Embrace every moment with Love.

All is one and returns.

# In Violet

In Violet you bathe.
In its soft glow is
your healing,
your awareness,
your reassurance.

In presence of Spirit,
in depth of excitement,
a calm flow emerges.
Be still, friend.
Breathe deeply.
In each breath,
we flow with you.

Within,
you are awakened.
Stay calm.
Still your mind.
Sense this moment.
We are close now.

Write freely.

Allow our words,
to mentor you within,
to guide you within,
to inspire you within.

You called on an Angel.
In Violet she came.

This color is yours,
my friend.
Your Angel,
as always,
is in waiting.

In this moment,
open to my energy.
I will guide thee.

When we call you to work,
my friend,
do not hesitate.
Trust in our words.
Creativity carries you to your Destiny.

Breathe gently, my friend.
Calm thyself.
This is truly happening.
We are at one.

Put aside conscious thought,
intellectual logic,
and your doubt.

As many sleep,
so, you are awakened.
Stand, fast, in your knowing.

Be still.

This moment is passing.

Our thoughts are now in words.
Reflect on them, my friend.
Seek their guidance.
Trust.
All will be well.

# Angel Of Love

Your Angel of Love is around you.
Her Light embraces you.
In her heart, she searches
to rest,
to connect,
to be with you.

Much time has passed.
Many journeys,
much searching,
self-debate.

Her glow feels warm.
She wishes
to bring Love to earth,
to settle to ground,
to rest her wings.

Through the love of Atlantis,
Heavens reflect on life.
Destiny reminds us,
her divine Light has a mission.

Take a moment, my friend,
to sense,
to understand,
to honour.

Divinity is intervening.

Your Angel has a duty to fulfill.
Your Angel brings comfort to Spirit.
Your Angel calls those awakened
to assist.

More Spirit on earth,
more Love on earth,
more Light on earth.

Embrace this, my friend.

Her duty dispensed,

this is truly a Moment in a Universe.

# In Ego

In Ego
you own all you possess.

In Truth
you own nothing.

In Ego
you are responsible
for all you possess.

In Truth
You are responsible
for nothing.

In Ego
you make your plans.

In Truth
these plans
have already been made.

In Ego
you seek Comfort
in your possessions.

In Truth
your Comfort lies within Love.

In Ego
you seek to stem your tears of sadness.

In Truth
these are tears of your teacher's lessons.

In Ego
you resent your fears.

In Truth
there are no fears to resent.

In Ego
wealth may purchase freedom.

In truth
Freedom is priceless.

In Ego
you search for more.

In Truth
you value what you have.

In Ego
you feel a need to be right.

In Truth
It can be right to be wrong

In Ego
all is different.

In Truth
all is One.

Within your darkness you will find Light.
Where there is Light there cannot be dark.
This Light is you,
as you wish to be.

n your darkness are many Colours.
_ook closely and you will see.
Silently watch, as colours come forth,
each hue the essence of you.

As you set yourself free,
see all that you wish to be,
can be and will be.

# You Will See

As you give with good intent,
so, you will receive,
in abundance,
more than you have perceived.

You are awakening to your Soul,
to your higher self.
You have opened to Spirit.
Feel fear subside as you bathe
in unconditional Love.

You and your Soul are at one.
You and a universe are at one.
The Light of Love is with you.
In Belief,
you have found, in yourself,
Peace and Joy.

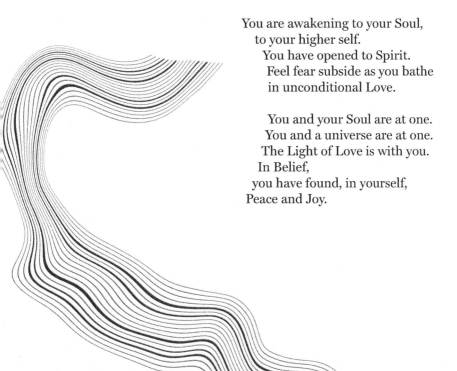

# Gentle Soul

Gentle Soul
that lies within my reach,
guide Spirit to my Destiny.

Comfort, Love and Nurture me.
Shine your Light within.

In this moment,
heal me,
enlighten me.

We are one.

As my tears flow
I sense thee, to my left.
In Spirit you guide me.
Your teachings become clearer.

My Angel surrounds me,
showing my path,
lighting my way.

My Angel swims in Joy
as,
with each breath,
we become closer.

Gentle Soul,
that lies within my reach,
let Love be our eternal bond.

# Child And Soul

Seek Love,
 in all your thoughts and deeds.
 Give for no return.
 Give forth as you would so desire.
 In Truth,
 Your needs will be returned.

In this moment,
feel Love around you,
your gentle heart racing,
energies, within your room
 am to your left.

ee Love in others.

n your lessons you have found Freedom.
Carry these lessons to others.

Do not judge others
 nor talk ill of them.
 Embrace them, see the oneness.

Bring to them the understanding.

Love and Freedom will be theirs.

Least not forget
the miracle of Birth,
nor Divine intervention of Soul
 as a creation of Love and Joy.

Know each Soul has its Destiny.
 From the union of Child and Soul
 lessons of Life commence.

We have much work to do,
 many souls to enrich,
 bringing Light to those in darkness,
 leading them to Joy in life,
 to the true
 union
 of child and soul.

I am to your left.

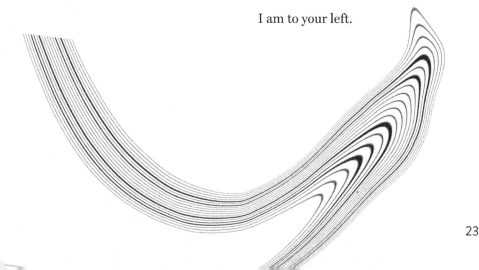

# Where Did You Go To

In night passed did you travel alone
in sight, sound and feelings?

Can you recall places?
People,
conversations,
our Love shared with you?

My friend,
many have visited you.
We have exchanged many words,
given much guidance,
unfolding within, as Joy.

Look into darkness,
with Light, see no fear.

When our meeting is passed,
we will call you to work.
You are prepared within, my friend.
Foundations are laid.

In those moments,
when we are at one,
lock away your intellect.

You will see.
You will, still, be.

You have journeyed far and know our ways.
You are loyal to them, my friend.

Know, in Truth,
as you bathe in our collective Wisdom,
in Love you are bountiful.

In Spirit, we work with you.
Follow our guidance.

# This Day

This day her journey begins.
Her kind heart lays bare.
As she embraces Spirit more closely
her Soul is awash with calm.

Her journey is measured not of Time
nor of distance.
Her journey is within,
to oneness and peace.

Within a universe
Angels are with her
in abundance and full of Love,
to guide and Light her way.

As a child embraces life,
she accepts this moment unconditionally,
sharing great Joy.

In Truth,
she will prosper.

In Truth,
she will learn.

In Truth,
she will know Love in abundance.

In Truth,
she will know,
we honor her this day.

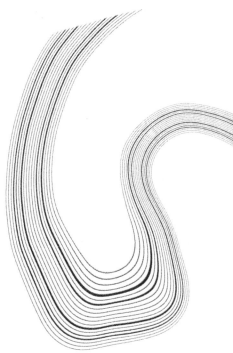

# Listening

Are you listening, my friend?

Do not dismiss your thoughts.
They are not invented.
You are not mind – wandering.
In each thought you have,
is meaning.

Listen for them.
Stay alert.
Write them down.
Trust me, my friend.
Follow my words.

I am guiding you.
I am lighting your way.
In Truth, you will find revelation
calling you closer to oneness.

I am pleased you stopped resisting today.
I have been talking to you for some Time.
In this moment, contemplate my voice.

Fear not.
In this Time we are close.
Calm thyself.

It is Truth.
It is Wisdom.
I am with Love.

# Is Eternity within?

Tell me what you hear
in this moment.

Are you listening, alert?
Can you sense
that which is called Eternity?

Look now my friend,
with your eyes closed.
I am in abundance.
Come closer to me.

In eternal Light you will grow.
As you bathe in its essence,
take time, my friend.
Come closer to me.
In our moments,
you will clearly see,

Reach out to me.
We are one.
Love is our circle of Light.

an image, a shadow, a light,
a feeling, a thought,
a silent voice in your mind.

Take ease.
Do not trouble to keep me.
Trust I will be.
Give yourself to the higher source.

What do you truly see
as you sense Eternity?

As our energies meet,
we are one.

Are you listening, alert?

Can you sense
that which is called Eternity?

Is eternity within?

# My Friend

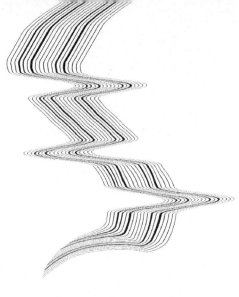

It is me.
Do not be fearful,
simply listen.

I am not in judgment,
I am here with Love.
Many times,
we have talked in the past,
when you sought reassurance.

In your wisdom you are learning
all answers truly lay within.
Put away your fears,
look to your life hereon.

Much is in store for you,
my friend,
you are not alone on this journey,
we are beside you.
Our Wisdom,
our Love will guide you.

Have faith.
When you were young,
we helped you believe in yourself.

Enjoy your Life, carry not guilt.
All you have, you are worthy of.

Treat yourself kindly.
Nurture yourself.
Honor yourself.
Last night as you slept
we were with you.
You know this,
you sensed us,
you saw us in your darkness,
briefly, but clearly.

All around you
wish you Joy,
here and on earth.

Our words
guide you and others.
Be not fearful.

Work in the moment.

We feel your love for us.
We feel your loss of us.
We are all with you, still.

Listen to silent voices.

We will call you to write.

Reflect on lessons given to you.
Your inner wisdom is awakened.

I sense in you, now,
calmness.
You are a cocoon of Light.

In the moment,
In the now,
be, still.

# Doubt

Doubt is with you my friend,
I know this.
I have been calling to you
for two days.

Fear not your thoughts.
They are real,
all will be well,
all is on course.

Resent not your doubt,
resent not your Self.

Your feelings are real.
They come from ego.

Ego,
will continue to be heard,
my friend, that is its job.

Ego begets darkness.
Truth begets Light.

You are in the Light, my friend,
Fear not.
Truth will win through.
Truth will conquer.

In them we will all bathe.

Go now,
further into the Light.

Enjoy these precious times
with love in your heart,
compassion and empathy.

Your Angel is rejoicing.

We are one.

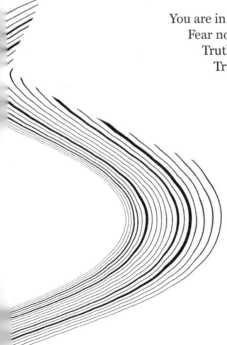

Fear not,
Light is guiding your path.
In Light you are free.

I am close, my friend,
to your left.

Your lessons are from Spirit.
Cast aside your doubts.
Ego will learn.

Tears of Joy will flow.

# Your Path Is Clear

In this moment how do you truly feel?
Do you feel in Truth?
Can you face this moment,
as you must?

If, in Truth, the answer is fearful,
cast that fear aside,
for, as your time moves by,
the answer will not change.

What pride is keeping you
from accepting who you are?

It is time, my friend, to let go.
This struggle is tiresome for you.
Capture this Truth that lies beneath,
in yourself, and in Destiny.

Be in Truth with your thoughts.
The Freedom you seek is within.
You are not bound or tied,
except by your own ego.

Listen to silent voices.
Reflect on these words.
Read all that we, together,
have brought to paper.

Be guided by them.

All will be clear.

It is time now to end your struggle.
You have much to do.

We leave you now, with Love.

Friend, put aside your fears,
those feelings in your stomach
of dread.
All will be well.

Quell those aches with Light and Love.
Within your soul lies Wisdom
always within your reach.

Friend, do not question this.
Simply be still.
Listen with all your senses.
Breathe deeply.
You can sense my being.
I am here.

A while ago I caught you
as you fell within.
For release, you sensed the need
to write.
This you know.

In rest, today, we have talked.
You have journeyed far.
Wisdom was shared with you.
In this moment you are overwhelmed.
You are questioning the path,
that awaits you.

Your journey is not to stand still
but to grow,
in Spirit,
in Light,
and
in Truth.

# Cast Fears Aside

Friend,
have no doubt
of your Destiny.

We will meet many times.
Be alert to my calling.

Today, you are feeling ungrounded.
Friend, you are anchored.
Your guides, your angels,
will hold you, fast.
Joy, Love and Peace are within.

When sands shift
we will support you.
Friend, have Faith.
We are with you.

Breathe deeply,
embrace us.
Sense our being,
our energy about you.
We will not let you fall.

We are to your left.

# Faith

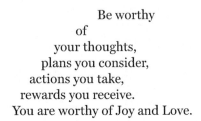

Wisdom
chooses one path,
confusion travels many.
However, my friend,
it makes sense to journey
before making the final choice.

In your journeys
many lessons will be learned,
difficult, sometimes joyful.
Do not judge yourself.
In life there are no mistakes,
simply lessons.
This is Truth.

Be worthy
of
your thoughts,
plans you consider,
actions you take,
rewards you receive.
You are worthy of Joy and Love.

With fixed opinions and answers
many judge and work in ego.
Many measure time.
Friend, Time in Truth does not exist.
We are eternal.

Loved ones are here.
They smile and send their Love.
Now
they are at rest and with much energy.
They feel your Love for them.

Allow yourself not to be caught in chaos.
Life is not a race to collect and hoard.
In essence, all that is made by man
was, first, a thought
and all of Nature
created by the Universe.

Take a moment, now.
Reflect on our words.

Guidance is with you.
Love is in abundance.
Sleep well tonight, friend.

Friend, align yourself to Nature.
Let it heal, nurture, and energize you.

I leave you with Love.

Heed my words.
Keep a journal.
Enter your thoughts.
Reflect on them.
Trust them.
They will guide you well.

Reflect on them.
Trust them.
Words will guide you well.

Where there is Light
there cannot be dark.
Nurture the Light workers' way,
my friend.
Embrace it with Love.
You shall receive, in return,
most bountiful.

# The Child

When next you look to the stars,
look to the one that shines brightest.
Feel light fill your heart.
Sense your universe.
Sense your connection.

Feel energies around you
in the moment.
Open your Heart and Soul to
them.
Breathe deeply as you look with
wonder.
As a child, many times,
you would look,
in awe of the vision.

Be now that child again
as you
channel the power,
harness the energy,
harvest the beauty around you.

Feel the Love of a Universe.
You are connected
to this and all of Mankind.

Life is a universe,
eternal,
of seas, earth and seasons,
to be
nurtured,
appreciated,
valued
and
respected.

Know the child again
who sees and senses no barriers,
to whom all is transparent.

Connect to this, my friend.
Awaken the child within.
Take this Wonder you have rediscovered,
bathe in it, share it and enlighten others.
See now, all that you truly have.

Be now that child again

and see.

# Honour Yourself

In this moment, you now understand
it is about you, my friend.
It has no accord to anyone else.
You realise, now, my friend,
it is time to honour yourself.

To Honour is to Respect.

Respect is your next move
towards your spiritual Destiny.
This is the path
of Light to your future.
It is not too late of years.
Remember, we have no such parallel,
we have no such measure as Time.
Put this aside now, my friend.
Move on.

It is clear, now.
You cannot be in any denial.

Denial of what you must do.
All journeys are of process,
with no short cut from pain,
nor avoidance of fear
but consider not, fear of failure.

My friend, Light your path.
Commence this journey.
Within a season,
you will change your perception
of your remaining life years
on earth.

You have had warnings.
You have had clear communications.
Today you have had
the most luminous communication.
A visitor was sent to you.

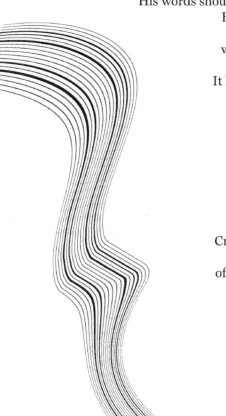

His words should be heeded
His words of self,
conveyed thoughts
we needed you to hear.

It has taken you many hours
to understand
the substance of his visit,
the purpose,
the Love.
that has brought him to you.

My friend,
do not use the word coincidence.
All thoughts are fruit of creation.
Create your future, as you want it to be.
Let go
of your physical and emotional shackles.

Much Love is with you.
We will guide you.
We will communicate, suggest,
give you options,
of creative thought.
You, my friend, make your choices.

Keep the Love.
You give so freely
Compassion,
Empathy
and
Understanding.

Now, my friend,
commence that Honour of you.
Think in Truth.
Shine bright in the Love you bathe in.
Share this Light with all,
for we are one.

I leave you, now, with Love.

# Spirit Works

You seek guidance.

Embrace your learning, my friend,
to reshape our words and those of others.
Work hard at this.
Be always respectful of the journey.
Stay within your integrity and purpose.

Your work will be for that of Spirit.
Your work will be in sharing, in awakening.
Still yourself, be of no haste.
Take much Time for debate.
Your Wisdom will guide your words.

Consider all in your thoughts,
from the fledgling to the seasoned.
Pour Love on those who may scorn,
or,
in their envy, be hurting.
Embrace them.
Their angels will heal them.
They will not be abandoned.

Continue your work with purpose, my friend.
Keep your Faith in us.
We are waiting.
Seek our guidance.
We will not fail you.

We are all connected.
In awakening you have brought Light to many

Look not for proof.
Simply be.
Look not for glory.
Simply be.

I am to your left.

# Words

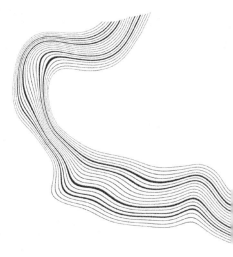

You have travelled many life times.
In those life times, my friend,
I have walked beside you,
as I do now.

As your writing progresses,
from beginning to end,
so, will our journey.

Read these words,
not once,
not twice,
but three times.

Understand their wisdom.
Light is with you,
Love is with you.

Your friend, who works with spirit,
will find her path within.
Do not concern yourself
over such moments as this.

I have been calling to you
for this conversation.

I am of age my friend.
Bring to your mind now,
that of oriental life.
Bring to your life
all that supports the item
you decided to hold today.

Your friends have worked hard for us,
to bring us to this point.
Forget them not in your love.

Work now so that we become closer.
Trust your intuition.
Be alert to Silent Voices.
Dismiss no thoughts.
Listen.

For in your close attendance,
will be your guidance.

Now, my friend, I will go,
trusting in your judgement,
your intuition,
your intellect,
your wisdom.

Begin this next journey my friend
with joy in your heart.
As I, in this moment, feel joy.

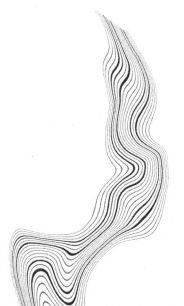

# Sensing Spirit

Silent Voices
are in much Joy.

In this moment you are aware of us.
Our ways are becoming closer to you.

Be aware of our energy around you.
Feel it, sense it, bathe in it.

Feel change, in this moment,
in your Spirit,
in your Heart
and
in your Soul.
Feel
Harmony within.

This, my friend, is yours in
abundance,

From within, Wisdom calls you.
Listen carefully.

Be alert to its whisper.
Be guided, my friend.
You walk in the light workers´
path.

All are joyful for you.

Today much will unfold for
you,
in your heart and in your
Spirit.
Be not, conscious of this.
You will see.
We are all as one.
Open to silent voices
of your Soul
my friend.

In your awakening
you will experience much joy.
We know you now carry no fear of us.

We hold your trust and understanding.
This brings us much closer to you,
my friend.

Wrap fear in Light.
In Light fear will disperse.
Live your life in Joy.

Embrace all around you
with your Wisdom.

Share this.
Heal with this.
Comfort and encourage with
this.
For your Soul asks this of you.

We leave you now with Love.

Be alert to our calling.
We have much to do,

I am to your left.

# This Night

Listen to me in this moment.
All will be well, my friend.
Your careful steps are
in the right direction.
You are back on your path, in Light.
Your destination is of good.

Your Wisdom is with you, my friend.
Your Soul is in Truth.
All will be well.
You sense me tonight.
Trust in this.

Our energies are attuned.

Enjoy now your
walking meditation,
working meditation,
silent meditation.

This is your path.
No intellectual thoughts are needed,
no rationale required.
Your higher self calls for these actions.
Silent voices will be heeded.

We are pleased with you,
for honouring us in your thoughts,
in your endeavors
to stay connected.

We ask nothing of you.
We make no judgment.
Be kind to yourself.

Some streams flow faster than others,
each stream following its own path,
confronting barriers and obstacles,
creating its course.

You may sit by the slowest stream,
to observe, to meditate upon it.
In this meditation,
you, too,
will confront your barriers and obstacles.

In these moments you will see clearly
the Creator of them is indeed Self.
Take time, my friend.

Do not press to make things happen.
See waters flow in their Time,
at their speed
as Nature has intended.

You will find, my friend, in Time,
you will be in the fastest flowing stream,
only to observe,
it is not the forceful water
you first thought,
but is equally
as gentle and deliberate in its journey,
as the slowest you had observed.

Sleep well, this night.
For tomorrow will be truly enlightening.
Tomorrow marks a moving forward
in your spiritual journey.

# We Are Close

We are of many life times.
We have journeyed before.
Many lessons we have learned.

In Truth, we work together.
In Truth, we grow closer.
Listen well, my friend.

Your journeys are not of Time,
for Time is not of consequence.
We are eternal.
All is of Energy.
All is connected.

Many times, in sleep, you
transcend,
travel many distances,
experience much Wisdom
and
share many intuitions.
Friend, on these journeys,
your power of perception grows.

Consider not Memory, nor Time,
to be of significance.
In your earth life they have
purpose,
in Spirit they are not of
substance.

In your precious
moments,
we are with you.
In your moments
of doubt and fear,
we are with you.

Fear is part of your life journey
and of lessons learned,
adding another layer
to
your precious Soul.

I say to you, my friend,
reach to your Soul.
Talk to your Soul as a friend.

As you come closer together
Joy,
Freedom
and
Harmony
will shine within.

Now, as you write your words
feel the gentle change.
Feel a sense of calm and reassurance,
in every fibre within.

Healing is at work, my friend.
Continue your life in this Love.
You are worthy.

All are worthy.
Help all to seek Truth
through spiritual awareness.

# Work With Us

Do not deny
the changes you are
experiencing.

Come with us now, my friend,
we are asking you.
This is real.
Silent Voices,
are calling to you from Spirit.

They are of a higher nature
than you have ever experienced,
within your
physical, emotional and spiritual being.
Fear not these shifts in awareness.
Show gratitude and reverence for all.

Listen well,
see us now in violet,
sense our energies with you.
Your Soul is asking you to be free.
Release yourself today
of all shackles.

Life is eternal, my friend.
Your Soul, your Spirit,
are eternal.
All you are connected to,
in Love,
will never leave you.

Joy is all around you,
yet, you still resist.
In Spirit we have no physical form.
We are energies of free will,
and good intent.

All will still be.
You will still be.

Throw away fear, my friend,
wrap it in Light.
Feel the Love you have for others.
Trust the Love others have for you.

We travel further
than those in earth life.
We can be in many places at one time.
We can touch you in the moment,
of a breath.

All are one and all are connected.
In light you are harvesting Love,
for mankind and Nature.
Friend, within Nature lies Truth.

Our energies bathe in Violet.
This healing Light we send
to you.
Within this Light we are connected
to you.

Our next journey has begun.
You are on the path of Light.
No darkness can befall you
as you walk in Light.

Come to us in Faith.
Trust our Love.
We are reaching out to you,
accept this gift.

Listen for Silent Voices this day.

My friend,
we leave you now
with Love.

# A Gift From
# The Universe

So diverse,
at times supportive,
a reassuring conduit for love.

In our grief,
placed upon a casket of a loved one,
as a celebration to their life.

Lining the pathways of generations,
of joyful celebrations
of queens, kings, princes and paupers.

Delicately adorning a marital bed,
as an expression of eternal love.

Your infinite, timeless qualities,
emblems of honour, courage and achievement
in times of conflict, adversity and peace.

Your endurance, standing fast to the extremes of nature's seasons,
achieving perennial Life.

So elegantly placed above your barbed and briary stem,
your vibrant fragrances seduce and inspire our senses.

One could ask why
such abundance of beauty,
is embroidered
amongst a tortured, and tormented, body,

Of such heritage,
ours is not to question,
but
instead,
to rejoice in the universal gift,
of our beloved rose.

# No Title

I wish to bring your attention,
to the ocean, to the Atlantic.
Spend more time my friend near these waters
that surround you.

Become much more aware
of their meaning.
For here you were meant to be,
my friend.

I am of much age.
I have experienced many life
journeys.

It is of no coincidence,
that you should choose
this item that you hold today.
This has been with you some time,

chosen of your own free will
on a special day.
It is significant, my friend.

Many have helped us
to come to this moment.
They have done good work,
for they knew the fears you have had
of spirit in any form.

Now we know such fears have gone,
you see us as friends.
You have learned
the wisdom of patience.
You have learned
to stand back from the storms.

Philosophy is not new to you,
my friend through many of your
lives
philosophy has been a running
thread.

Your family and friends are
well,
they send their love to you today.
They have joy on their faces,
they are contented.

I will wait for you now, my friend
as you progress in our ways,
developing our disciplines.
I shall become closer to you.

You have commented many times
you are too old to embark
on a spiritual journey.
Fear not of your age.

My friend, in spirit time is of no consequence.

For we all return as one,
you have much time.

# Moving On

Integrity, Wisdom and Trust,
we share.
In our teachings,
we are all one.

In harmony, ego rests.
Within self, you are finding peace,
you know we are closer.

You are alert to my thoughts,
in activity,
in sleep,
in rest,

No more doubt.
You know,
all before you is complete.
You are in the now.

Adversity has taught you lessons.
Through this you are closer to self.
In this you feel secure.

No longer do you question, my friend.
Instead,
you know, to be in the now
is all you seek.

In meditation,
your vibrations will be raised.
Attune yourself through slight change.
Do not work hard in this process.

Let it be.
Let it flow.
You will see.

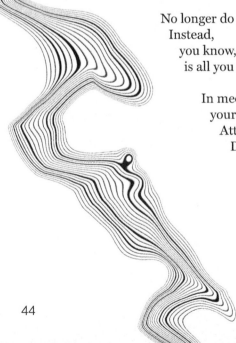

# Freedom

Trawling through life's rivers of change,
seeking currents of least resistance,
absorbed into the fullness of each day,
reflecting on past challenges.

Have I lived my life that way?

As tides of life flow high and low,
how much more do I really know?

Did I truly grow?

At times my rivers have raged like a storm
settling to moments of magical insights,
guiding me to Joy.

In the corridors of my mind,
itineraries of times gone past.
Memories as rich resilient cameos,
now fading so fast.

Adjusting for tranquillity and peace,
navigating no more the uncertain tiring rivers of life,
no wind in my sails but resting on a calm lake.

My once vice like grip,
now a feather, floating to rest.
No more pain or fear,
just a gentle, loving, embracing peace.

Freedom is finally here.

Printed by Amazon Italia Logistica S.r.l.
Torrazza Piemonte (TO), Italy